GPS for Presentations

A structured approach to planning presentations with a clear message and focused content

Dave Paradi

Other books by Dave Paradi:

Select Effective Visuals
Present It So They Get It
The Visual Slide Revolution
102 Tips to Communicate More Effectively Using PowerPoint
Guide to PowerPoint (editions for PowerPoint 2003, 2007 and 2010)
Delivering Your Message With PowerPoint

Published in Canada and the United States
by Communications Skills Press.

ISBN 978-0-9881549-2-6

Printed in Canada and the United States of America

www.GPSforPresentations.com

Cover by Rebecca Renner of Creative Minds Inc.

PowerPoint® is a registered trademark of Microsoft Corporation.

Contents

Acknowledgements

GPS for Presentations

A structured approach to planning presentations with
a clear message and focused content

CHAPTER ONE

Improving Presentations is critical to business & personal success

Why do business professionals need a new approach for creating presentations? Because presentations are an increasingly important part of every business professional's job and the current approaches that most professionals use don't work well. In this chapter I want to review some of the background to set the stage for the GPS approach that is the focus of the rest of the book.

Presentations are becoming the de facto method of communicating in organizations

If you feel that you are attending more presentations and delivering more presentations in your role as a business professional, you are not alone. In the surveys I do of audiences, I have seen a steady rise in the number of people who report that they see at least one PowerPoint presentation each day as part of their role. In fact, the percentage of people who reply to my surveys that report daily presentation viewing has more than doubled in the last eight years.

Presentations have become the de facto way of communicating in organizations today. When I report these statistics in my customized workshops, I get agreement from almost every attendee. They have been asked to create more presentations and they see more presentations each year. Whether you think this is a positive trend or not really doesn't matter. This is the reality in organizations today.

Oral communication is a key business skill according to executives

Well known entrepreneur Richard Branson said that "Communication is the most important skill any leader can possess." No matter what level you are at in an organization, communicating effectively is a critical skill. Communicating to staff, peers, executives, vendors, suppliers, customers, and other stakeholders is essential. A survey of over 330,000 business professionals reported in Inc. magazine showed that "Communicates powerfully and prolifically" is in the top five of leadership skills required to succeed today.

As you move up in an organization, effective communication becomes even more important. An article in Harvard Business Review on the same large survey went deeper to explain that as leaders move into senior management roles, the communication skill moves into the top two leadership skills essential for success. A separate HBR article reporting on a survey of senior consultants at a top executive search firm reported that "Communication and presentation" was one of the top skills companies look for when recruiting executives.

So it is not just our audiences who think presentations need to be well done, but leaders and executives are looking at this skill as increasingly important to the future of the organization.

Presentations are costing organizations more than they realize

Why should organizations invest in improving the way presentations are created? Because there is a bottom line benefit when they do so.

The current methods of creating presentations are costing organizations far more than they realize:

- Professionals spend many hours each week creating presentations, often using inefficient methods that waste time and effort.

- Many hours are wasted each day by professionals who have not been taught efficient ways to create slides in PowerPoint, the tool they are required to use.

- Organizations waste hours each week sending versions of PowerPoint files back and forth in review.

- Ineffective presentations lead to delayed decisions and missed opportunities.

- Managers spend hours at night and on weekends revising the slides their staff create so the message is clear before presenting to executives.

How much, in dollars, is being wasted? Every organization will be unique, but it is not hard to calculate potential savings in the hundreds of thousands of dollars for a single division of a company. One of my clients did a Return on Investment calculation on one of my workshops. They only looked at the time saving in planning the presentation and creating the slides in PowerPoint. They found that the cost of flying everyone in for the two-day workshop, the employee time, and my costs would be paid back in under two months, just from the time savings the participants initially identified.

Improving presentations isn't just about getting better at a required skill, it has a positive bottom line impact for organizations as well.

Why so many presentations are described as "boring"

If presentations are so important, why do so many people say that most presentations are boring? In my survey of audience members the word "boring" is by far the most common word people use when describing the presentations they see in their organizations. I don't think any presenter intends to create a boring presentation.

Here's how I think it happens. It starts when we overload the presentations with information. This could show up as spreadsheets on slides, paragraphs of text, or diagrams that are too complex. When the audience sees this overload of information, they get confused. They are not sure what they are supposed to get out of it all. Should they try to figure out the slides or listen to the presenter? How do they find what the presenter is speaking about on the slides?

After a short time, they mentally check out. They might still be there physically, but mentally they have left the room. They start thinking about other things and may even start working on their phone, tablet, or laptop. By the end of the presentation, they say they are bored because it has been so long since they got anything of value from the presentation.

The old advice of "Tell Them" three times doesn't work

There is a classic piece of advice that many presenters have heard when thinking about how to structure their presentation. The advice is to: "Tell them what you are going to tell them, tell them, then tell them what you told them." I don't think this advice works anymore. Audiences expect better.

If you simply repeat your message three times, it ends up coming off as confusing if the audience thinks that there are actually three different points. If the audience recognizes the three points as the same ones, this approach comes off as condescending because the audience thinks that you consider them not intelligent enough to understand it the first time. Neither of these audience reactions will get you to your goal of having the audience understand and act on your message.

So what should you do instead? Use the GPS approach in this book to plan your message. If you want an updated version of this classic advice, I would suggest: Tell them the conclusion, Tell them how you justify the conclusion, and Tell them what you want them to do with the conclusion.

This matches well with the GPS approach in this book. It starts by letting the audience know where you are going, or the destination. It explains the steps you want them to take from where they are now to reach the conclusion you want them to reach. And it makes sure you have their commitment to act on the conclusion.

The typical approach of Grab & Hope doesn't work

Every business professional I speak to is very busy these days. Since the economic turmoil of 2008-9, almost every corporate professional is essentially doing two jobs due to downsizing and not adding staff when the business grew. Time is at a premium and people are looking for the fastest way to get things done.

When most professionals have to put together a presentation, they default to what they have always done, and what they have seen their colleagues do. They start by grabbing slides from previous presentations, theirs and ones done by colleagues, and throw them into a file. They then start trying to figure out how this will flow coherently. They add some slides when they think it might help or if a topic is missing. They hope it all comes together before they have to present it. I call this the Grab and Hope method.

To borrow a line from Dr. Phil, "How's that working for you?" Most professionals just chuckle when I describe this common approach. They know this is what they do. It isn't working well, but they don't know what else to do.

The solution is to spend time up front planning the message first. Use the GPS approach described in this book. Once you know what topics and information you need, then decide if there are slides or other content that will work to present the messages you have planned. Add any slides that you need to, and arrange it according to the plan.

Advice for speakers doesn't apply to business professionals who present

I regularly see articles with advice for speakers. It could be five things to do, nine things to avoid doing, or some variation on those themes. You probably see these articles too. You can safely ignore almost all of this advice. Let me explain why.

The problem with these articles is that they don't apply to the vast majority of business presenters. These articles are written for professional speakers who give inspirational keynote presentations to audiences in ballrooms. If you see words such as: stage, AV crew, lighting, crowd, microphone, or sponsors in an article, the advice doesn't apply to you.

I would guess that 95+% of all presentations given each day are by business professionals whose primary job is not speaking, but providing service to their organization and clients. They are not presenting on a stage in front of a large crowd. They are presenting to a few people in a meeting room trying to convince them to take a specific action. The context is totally different to a professional speaker.

There are three specific differences that make most of the advice for professional speakers invalid for business professionals who deliver presentations: the goal, the setting, and the audience.

Goal: A professional speaker is there to inspire the crowd, make them feel good, and have an enjoyable time. There is not a specific action that the entire crowd needs to agree with and act on. A business professional needs to communicate a clear message that results in action by the small group of people in the room. When these articles talk about using inspirational stories and full screen images, ignore that advice.

Setting: The professional speaker is on a large stage in a huge room with lights and professional AV. A business presenter is in a typical meeting room that has a projector or flat screen TV. Advice about microphones, staging, and AV crew don't apply. As a business professional, be prepared to deal with any technical issue on your own and keep things as simple as you can to reduce the risk that something goes wrong.

Audience: The large crowd listening to a professional speaker is very diverse, from those who are interested in the topic and speaker to those who are there because someone made them come. The professional speaker focuses on generalities because of this. A business professional has only a few key people in the room. They are there because they are a decision maker or key stakeholder. They won't waste their time in a meeting if they are not required. They are there to debate, give input, and make decisions. A business presenter needs to be focused on the topic at hand and be specific to give this audience what they need.

As a business professional who presents, you need to read articles for speakers with a critical eye. Much of it doesn't apply to you. Focus on the advice that will apply to your situation, and discard the rest.

What audiences want presenters to do better

In my last survey of audiences I asked them what advice they would give presenters on how to create and deliver more effective presentations. After reviewing all of their suggestions, the most important advice they have for presenters is to be clear: clear on the message, clear slides, and clear delivery.

Audiences expect the presenter to have defined the goal of the presentation. Too often the presentation is just a collection of slides that don't seem to have any purpose. Audiences consider this a waste of their time. Presenters need to consider the audience they will be speaking to and what that audience needs to hear. Don't tell them all you know. Carefully select just the points that will help deliver the important message you want them to remember when they leave. If you are asking someone to attend a presentation, make sure they will find it a worthwhile investment of their time. The GPS approach in this book is focused on helping you create a clear, concise message.

Once you have planned a clear message, the audience wants every slide you use to be clear as well. More than a few respondents advised presenters to limit themselves to only one point per slide. Have a headline that summarizes the message and an effective visual instead of a slide full of text. We will discuss how the GPS approach leads to creating this type of slide for your presentation.

When it comes to delivering the presentation, audiences want it to be clear and polished. Many comments were made about presenters stumbling through their content and apologizing to the audience. This can be avoided if you rehearse your presentation. When you know your content and your slides well, you will also avoid facing the screen and reading the slides. This drives audiences crazy and they desperately want presenters to stop wasting their time by reading out loud what could have been just sent by email.

A fundamental shift in approach is needed

I believe that a fundamental shift in the philosophy of presentation preparation is needed in order to dramatically improve the effectiveness of our presentations. When I ask someone why they have done something a certain way in their presentation, the answer I almost always get is, "We've always done it that way." It is what the person in the job before them did, it is what they see their peers and boss do, and they haven't seen any other way to create presentations. I don't think that approach is good enough.

I think we need to move to an approach of deliberate decisions. There should be a specific reason for the way we have done everything in our presentations. This shift in philosophy questions everything and makes us think about why certain content, visuals, and techniques will be effective for this presentation. It gives us more confidence that what we create is the best it can be.

This shift changes the way you prepare your presentation, which is the focus of this book. It changes the way you think about the volume of content in your presentation, another topic we will cover. It changes how the slide is planned, with a headline and an effective visual. And it changes what visual we select, the topic of my book *Select Effective Visuals*.

I encourage you to embrace the deliberate decision approach and think about every aspect of your presentation differently. Start by using the GPS approach in this book. The result will be more effective presentations that you will be more confident delivering.

The benefit to improving your approach to presentations

Using the GPS approach in this book will save you time in creating presentations. I know it initially sounds like it will take more time because it is adding steps in preparing your presentation. Compared to the typical Grab and Hope approach described above, the participants in my workshops say they save time overall.

By doing the planning up front, you reduce the time spent selecting previous content because you know exactly what you need and can decide if a previous slide will work or you need to create a new slide. The Grab phase goes much faster when you know what you need to grab. The Hope phase is replaced by focused planning up front and focused creation of new slides and arranging. Together this takes far less time than the struggle of trying to fit different slides into a coherent message.

Participants tell me that this approach cuts the time they spend preparing presentations dramatically. Here's an example of how this can work.

Minutes spent on tasks to create a presentation using the two methods

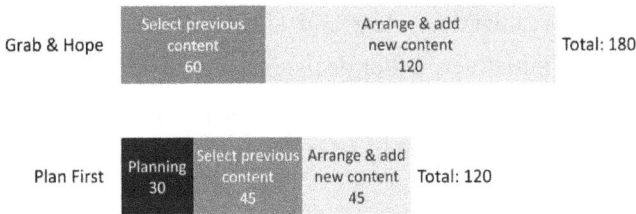

	Select previous content 60	Arrange & add new content 120	Total: 180
Grab & Hope			

	Planning 30	Select previous content 45	Arrange & add new content 45	Total: 120
Plan First				

There is no guarantee of how much time you will save, but people tell me that this approach cuts the time it takes them to prepare presentations, leaving more time for their other tasks. Next time you have to create a presentation, don't use the Grab and Hope method, try the GPS approach in this book.

Not only will you save time preparing presentations, your presentations will be more effective. How does this show up? One key measure is that you get fewer questions during and after your presentation. Some presenters think that more questions means that the audience is more interested. Often that is not the case. More questions are asked because they are confused. Fewer questions are asked because they understood your message clearly.

Another key indicator that your presentations are effective is that the audience takes action after you are finished. Confusion leads to delays in decision making and action, but clear communication allows action to be taken immediately.

The final indication that your presentations are effective is that you hear positive comments from peers and management. You start to be asked to present in front of more senior audiences or in public settings. And you will see a positive impact on your career trajectory.

As an organization, clear and effective presentations allow progress on initiatives, better decisions, and increased sales. The benefit of improving presentations is not just personal, but very significant when multiplied across the organization.

CHAPTER TWO

GPS for Presentations Overview

When I think of a presentation, I think of it as taking the audience on a journey. Today, almost everyone has used a GPS to help plan and take a trip. Whether it is a dedicated GPS device, one built into a vehicle, or an app on our smartphone, these systems give us a detailed plan for travelling between a starting location and our destination.

I started seeing this analogy apply to the planning of a presentation a few years ago. I started sharing parts of the idea with audiences and it resonated so well that I developed it further into a complete approach that can be used by any business professional to plan their presentation.

I redefined the acronym as follows:

G – Goal

A GPS starts by asking you the destination you want to reach. In our presentations, the destination is the goal of the presentation.

P – Present Situation

The next step in using a GPS is for it to determine your current location. In a presentation, this is determining the present situation the audience and the presenter find themselves in.

S – Steps

Once the GPS has your current location and your destination, it determines the best route for the chosen method of transportation. In a presentation, the steps are the topics, points, and supporting information we will use to move the audience from their present situation to the goal we set for the presentation.

As I examined this analogy in more detail, I saw more parallels between using a GPS and planning a presentation:

Focusing the content

A GPS only shows the step that you need to follow at that time. If you need more details, it has them available. In presentations, we need to do the same. We need to focus the content so that we do not overwhelm our audience. And we need to have the extra content the audience might ask about easily accessible.

Visually displaying one step at a time

When you use the directions from a GPS, it gives you one step at a time in a way that is easy to follow. In presentations we need to use effective visual slides that the audience can easily understand instead of spreadsheets and paragraphs of text.

The rest of this book goes into detail in each of these areas so you can use the GPS approach to plan your presentations.

CHAPTER THREE

Goal

When you are using a GPS for a trip, the first thing you need to do is tell the GPS your destination, the exact location you want to go. Without a destination, the GPS can't help you get there.

The equivalent of the destination in our presentation is the goal of our presentation, why we are creating this presentation. If we don't know why this presentation is being done, we have almost no chance of it being successful.

It is concerning that too many presenters don't actually know why they are creating the presentation. They tell me that it is because they do this presentation every month, or their boss asked them to prepare a presentation. To me, those aren't good enough reasons.

Sometimes a presenter will tell me what topic they are presenting. If you are only thinking about the topic, you haven't gone far enough. I suggest that the goal of your presentation also includes "why" you are presenting, in addition to "what" you are presenting. You aren't just presenting a project update, you are seeking management support (in terms of time, resources, and scope) to continue moving the project in a certain direction. You aren't just presenting the monthly financial analysis, you are presenting the insights that allow executives to make decisions that will positively impact future results.

A template for a clear presentation goal

One of the ways that I find helps presenters to really get clear about the goal of their presentation is to state the goal by completing this phrase: "At the end of the presentation the audience will _____." What will they know, what will they do, what will they understand, what will they agree to, what will they approve? What action do you want the audience to take at the end of your presentation? If there is no reason for the audience to attend because there is no clear goal, then perhaps you are really creating a memo, not a presentation. Email that to everyone and save them the time.

There are two tests I apply to check that a goal is clear.

Test #1: Is it specific?

The first test I apply is, "Is the goal specific?" Here I am looking for a way to measure the goal. As a presenter, how will you measure that you actually achieved the goal? If you can't measure it, it will be very hard to know whether you achieved the goal or not.

This is similar to using a GPS when planning a trip. If you enter just the city you are going to, it won't be able to direct you to the exact building. It needs a specific destination with the street number, street name, city, state, and zip code if you have it.

If your presentation goal is getting approval or reaching an agreement, those are easy to measure. Other types of presentations are not so easy. If you are presenting analysis of operational data, what are some possible goals? One common goal is to ensure that the management team understands the insights that you discovered in your analysis. You may not have any control over what decisions they make based on those insights, but you want to make sure you check with the audience during the presentation that they understand the conclusions you have drawn. This can be as simple as their heads nodding after you share a key insight. Or it could be a follow-up question that shows they understood and want to clarify one detail.

Test #2: Is it realistic?

The second test I apply is, "Is it realistic?" Is it realistic to achieve this goal in the timeframe and situation we are facing? If your goal is to get a decision but you don't have the decision maker in the room, it will be very hard to achieve that goal. If you have only been given ten minutes to explain a complex situation that has many sensitive aspects, it may not be possible to provide the depth of understanding required in the time that you have been allotted.

Again this is similar to how a GPS operates when planning a trip. The address you give the GPS software must actually exist. If you mistype the address, it gives you an error or attempts to guess what you really meant to type in.

Sometimes we think the goal is realistic, but don't realize that it is not until we complete the next step in this process, analyzing the present situation. So don't be concerned if you have to revisit the goal later on in planning your presentation.

It seems like completing the above template phrase would be easy, but in many cases it is harder than you think.

Let me share an example that illustrates how important it is to determine the correct goal for your presentation. A business owner named Bruce runs a small insurance agency in California. He came to me because he had a very important presentation coming up. He said, "Actually Dave, this is the biggest contract I've ever been up for. I'm down to the final two agencies for this contract." Bruce runs a small agency in the suburbs, just Bruce and a few staff. He said, "I'm up against one of the big agencies. They've got the glass office tower downtown, their name on the top. They are a big player." The Board of Directors of the organization was having a meeting and Bruce was to present before lunch followed by the competitor presenting their proposal.

I asked Bruce what he thought the goal of the presentation was. Bruce said, "Using your template: At the end of the presentation the Board of Directors will buy the policy from me." I next applied my two tests. First, is it specific? Can it be easily measured? Bruce's goal easily passed this test. Second, is it realistic? Can it be achieved in the time and situation? Here's where we ran into an issue. I said, "So it's about five minutes to noon Bruce, you're wrapping up your presentation. You've got your contract with the little yellow Sign Here sticky note on it. You slide the contract over to the Chair of the Board and ask for their signature on the binding contract. Is that going to happen?" Bruce had to admit that getting the Chair to sign the contract was not realistic because the Board had not even heard the competitor's presentation yet.

Now we had to go back and figure out the real goal of that presentation. This is a mandatory type of insurance in the state of California, and all policies expire on the same day each year. The organization Bruce was presenting to found themselves in a problematic position because their premiums had risen dramatically over the last three years and they didn't know why. They were paying a lot more for this mandatory insurance and wanted to bring the premiums down. The goal we came up with was that at the end of presentation, the Board of Directors would know how to make the decision on which proposal was best for this type of insurance.

Bruce specializes in this type of insurance. Bruce works with plenty of organizations who have found themselves in the exact same situation. We put together a presentation that explained why they were in this position of paying more each year. We explained what they had done (or not done) that had caused insurers to believe they were a higher risk, therefore raising their premiums. We explained how they could get out of the situation by following Bruce's three year plan. We showed case studies of other clients who were in the same position, and how they brought their insurance rates down by following Bruce's plan. So at the end of the presentation, the Board of Directors would be educated and know how to make this decision.

Bruce said that during the presentation he had really good interaction with the Board members. They asked questions and shared they were having lots of "a-ha" moments as they realized why they were in the current situation. At the end of the presentation they sincerely thanked Bruce. We knew that if we educated the Board, they would pick Bruce's proposal because it addressed the situation better. And sure enough the next day, Bruce got a call from the Board, "Bruce, we're going with your policy." It was the largest contract Bruce had ever won. Why?

One key factor was that we didn't accept the first statement of the presentation goal.

When you're creating presentations for others to deliver, getting clear on the goal is critical. You need to ask them to complete the template phrase above, "At the end of the presentation, where do you want the audience to be? what do you want them to know or understand? what decision do you want them to make?" After you ask, pause and wait for their answer. Don't be surprised if you get silence. Often they don't really know why the presentation is being done.

Just wait until they give you an answer that passes the two tests above. This will ensure that you don't waste your time creating a presentation that isn't what they wanted and they don't waste time making extensive revisions to what you created. And most importantly, you don't waste the audience's time sitting through a presentation that has no real goal or purpose (we've all sat through more of these type of presentations than we'd care to admit).

It is perfectly OK at this stage to decide that you need to communicate to a group but that a presentation is not the best vehicle for that communication. Perhaps a memo or a report is better than the huge cost of getting people together in a room.

Please don't skip this critical first step: determine a clear goal that is specific and realistic.

CHAPTER FOUR

Present Situation

Once you have your destination entered in the GPS, it then figures out where you are right now, your current location. It searches satellites, it looks at WiFi signals, cell tower signals, IP addresses, and other information to figure out where you are right now because it needs to have that starting point. And once it does that, most of the GPS systems give you the blue dot on the map, where you are right now.

In our presentations, the equivalent to the current location on the map is the present situation. I see two parts to evaluating the present situation when preparing a presentation: the audience and the logistics.

Roles in the audience

One of the aspects of the audience is the different roles that people have in that audience. This is especially important if you are in a situation where your goal relates to having a decision made, an approval, or an agreement. It's very important to understand who are the decision makers and who are the influencers. Influencers are those to whom the decision maker turns and says, "So what do you think about this?" Now, they aren't making the decision, but the decision maker trusts their judgement.

One of my clients outside Chicago actually has a sign stuck to the floor at the entrance of every meeting room and a circular sign hanging down in the middle of the room from the ceiling. It reminds people of the three roles they've identified for meetings: decision maker, influencer, and stakeholder. As a presenter, you are reminded, "I need to identify who those are." As people coming in, the participants in the meeting, you are reminded to remember what role you have. It is an interesting way to remind everybody to think of what role they play in this meeting.

Different levels of knowledge

The next aspect of evaluating the audience is to determine their level of knowledge about your topic, both real and perceived. There are some times when people think they have more knowledge than they actually do. If you believe this to be true, don't embarrass them by pointing this out. Incorporate phrases such as, "As you probably already know ...", to convey information without them losing face in front of their peers.

The biggest challenge for most presenters comes when you have an audience with different levels of knowledge. You have some people at one end of the spectrum where they really don't know much about the topic at all. Their concern is, "I'm going to be asked to contribute, to be part of this meeting. I really don't want to because I don't know anything about this topic and I'm going to look like a fool." Then you have people at the other end of the spectrum, the experts. They know a lot about this topic. They come into the room and they look around the room and they think, "Oh my gosh! Newbies. Why do we even let them in the room? We're going to waste half our time trying to explain the basics to these people."

If you are smiling right now, it is likely because you can relate to this situation. The question is how do we handle this wide variety of knowledge levels in the room? The best approach I have come up with is to start the meeting like this, "Folks, I want to just take the first five minutes and make sure we're all up to speed on the three areas we need to keep in mind in order to have a discussion and make decisions later on." What this approach does is limit scope and limit time.

I limit scope for the folks at the one end of the spectrum who don't know a lot about this topic because now they can relax thinking, "I don't need to be an expert in this topic. At least I'll know the three things we will be discussing so I can make a reasonable contribution." I limit the time for the folks at the other end of the spectrum so they know the explanation won't take half the meeting, it's just five minutes, and then we'll be able to have a better discussion. When you have a mixed audience, you have to figure out the minimum background information needed to ensure everyone can contribute and how to present it in the least amount of time.

Concerns will be addressed

You will want to do some research to find out what concerns or objections your audience has to what it is you're going to talk about. You may be aware of these if you regularly present to this group. You may need to ask others who have presented to this group what they have previously observed. And you may be able to ask one or more members of the audience directly. It is important to identify these concerns in advance if possible.

I learned the importance of this very clearly one time in Jacksonville, Florida. I was speaking to a conference of 150 invited Accounting professors. I was one of three concurrent speakers during one afternoon. They broke the large group up into three groups of 50, and these smaller groups rotated through the three breakout rooms spending about an hour in each. My first group was done and they left for their break. My second group starts arriving and a man comes in the door at the far end of the room, comes right towards me, gets right up in my face and passionately says, "Dave, I just want you to know I HATE PowerPoint!" There was no doubt about his concern! That was so valuable for me though. I started that session by saying, "Now, I understand that not everybody thinks that PowerPoint is useful for teaching accounting. What I want to do over the next 50 minutes is show you some specific examples of where I believe it will help your students understand the concepts you're teaching."

When you know there are concerns or objections in the room, let people know you will be addressing them during your time. You don't have to address them right up front. But if you let them know you will be addressing their concerns during the presentation, then at least they can relax knowing that their concern/objection will be addressed. If they don't know whether you will address the burning concern they have, you are likely to observe one of two behaviors. The first is they sit there with their arms crossed, a grimace on their face, and they don't listen to anything you say until you actually address that concern. The other behavior you get is from an executive in the room. If they haven't heard within the first two slides that you will be addressing their objection or concern, they jump right in and derail your presentation to make sure their concern gets addressed. The behavior you observe may depend on who is in the room. By saying right up front that you will be addressing these concerns in the appropriate way and sequence, you allow them to relax and pay attention to the whole presentation.

Logistics of the presentation

The other part of assessing the present situation is the logistics of the presentation. How will people be attending – in person, via the web, both? This is an important consideration because there are some techniques that work in person but do not work well for web based attendees. Does the presentation need to also stand on its own for those who could not attend? If this is the case, then you will need to incorporate more detail in the file that is sent out so that those who did not hear you speak still understand the key messages.

An emerging consideration is in what format any materials will be made available to attendees. More organizations today do not allow printed handouts because of their environmental policy. That means you will have to make sure the room is set up with power sources (if needed) and web connectivity for everyone to be able to access the handouts you want them to be able to refer to.

Your credibility with this group

Another factor you need to consider when assessing the present situation is how much credibility you have with this audience. If this is an audience you have spoken to many times before or they are very familiar with you, you may not need to do much in this area.

If you are new to this audience, you should consider how to introduce yourself so that they consider you a credible source of information from the start. Don't make the mistake of droning on about every aspect of your education and work past. Focus on what experience or education you have that is relevant to the topic and goal of the presentation. An effective introduction sets the stage for the presentation and explains how your presentation (and you) will benefit the audience.

When you are presenting with others in a multi-presenter presentation, don't make the mistake of sounding surprised that the next slide is to be presented by someone else and end up saying, "Oh, this is your slide Paul; I guess it's your turn now." This makes it sound like the presentation was thrown together at the last minute and is not coordinated (whether that is true or not).

In a multi-presenter situation, the introductions need to be brief to continue the flow of the overall presentation. The aim should be for 15 to 30 seconds or less. Here is an example:

"As compelling as the operational advantages of this initiative are, we know that you are also concerned about the financial impact of the work. I'd like to ask Paul to come and talk about the financial analysis he has done that shows how this project is a high return initiative. Paul has an MBA and has provided solid analysis that we have based our own decisions on for two years. Paul, walk us through this next section please."

There are a number of things to notice in this example:

1. There is a tie to the previous section. To give the audience context for why the next presenter should be speaking,

the previous presenter needs to set up why the next topic is relevant and important at this time in the presentation.

2. It positions why the audience should listen by previewing the key point that the next presenter will be speaking to. This gets the audience primed to listen to the support for the conclusion that they have been given.

3. It positions the next presenter as the expert in the topic by explaining that they are the ones who have done the analysis and their advice has been relied on in the past. It also gives any relevant education or external qualifications. If external qualifications are not available, reference internal ones.

4. It invites the next presenter to start right away with the topic at hand. The audience does not want to have breaks in the flow, so they want the presenter to get right to the points they are going to share.

These introductions should be practiced and rehearsed in advance. Don't think that you can just "wing it" on the day of the presentation. You will forget a part or forget to introduce the person at all. Also, don't just stumble through a printed introduction. If you need to read it because you won't be able to remember it, include it in your normal speaking notes and refer to it just like you would refer to your notes for any slide you are delivering. It should seem natural and flow like all the rest of your points. You are the one who will convince the audience that the next presenter is an expert.

A key component to making multi-presenter presentations effective is to develop and deliver the introductions so they create a smooth transition for the audience from section to section. Prepare for this part of your presentation just as you prepare for the content you will be delivering. It will make your presentation more effective and show how well your team works together.

CHAPTER FIVE

Steps

Once a GPS system knows your destination and your current location, it looks at all the different ways you can get from where you are to your destination. It considers traffic, time of day, construction, and other factors and determines the best route to get you from where you are to where you want to be. It starts by displaying a high-level overview of that route.

In our presentation planning, we use our knowledge of the subject area, our analysis of the present situation, and any other factors to determine the best way to move the audience from where they are now to the goal we have set for this presentation.

Topics

The high level view of our plan is the topics that we will cover. I like to use the analogy of the topics being like a physical set of stairs. If I walk up to a set of stairs and it only has three or four stairs, I think, "Oh, this is easy, I can get up this... " and up I go.

If you've ever been at the bottom of one of those circular staircases that go around and around, or the ones that go back and forth, back and forth and you look up and can't even see the end of the stairs, I don't know about you but I'm tired before I start. You are going to share these topics with your audience as the agenda. So be careful, please don't do what I saw a presenter do a few years ago. They sent me the slides for what was supposed to be a one hour presentation. The agenda was seven slides long! By slide four people are looking for a graceful way to get out of the room because that's going to be what's known as a "drinking from the fire hose" presentation. Just like you wouldn't want to climb too many stairs to reach the top, don't expect your audience to want to sit through too many topics during your presentation.

Topics help organize your presentation for the audience the way signposts organize your journey when using a GPS system. At the start of the trip the GPS system tells you the main signposts you will see and during the trip it prompts you to look for each sign to take the next part of the journey. In our agenda we share with our audiences the topics, or signposts that they can look for during the presentation. During the presentation I suggest you use signpost slides to let the audience know where they are in the presentation. A signpost slide has nothing except the phrase for the next topic. This phrase matches what the audience saw in the agenda at the start of the presentation. When the audience sees this phrase, they connect it back to the high-level outline of topics in the agenda and instantly have context for where you are in the presentation. Some presenters like to create signpost slides that are a copy of the agenda slide with the next topic highlighted, and this works as well. If you are concerned that this will add more slides to your presentation, it does add more slides, but not more time, as you are spending only a few seconds on these signpost slides. Those few seconds are helpful to keep the audience on track.

Points

The GPS system has more detail for each of the steps in the high-level overview of the journey. It will show you the detail that you need in order to complete your journey. Similarly, our presentation plan goes to the next level of detail by breaking the topics into specific points that you need to cover in order to move the audience from where they are now to the goal you set. You are an expert in your subject area, so you have the knowledge to break down the topics into points.

Within each topic, does it matter what sequence the points are presented in? Absolutely! A GPS system doesn't give you the directions in a random order, there is a sequence that makes sense. The points in each topic need to be in a sequence that makes sense.

Supporting information

We believe the directions the GPS system gives us because we implicitly trust the source of their information. If we get steered wrong by a GPS system, we start to question everything it gives us. In presentations, our audience doesn't just believe what we say implicitly. We have to support or prove our points. There are some effective ways to support each point.

The first is to use published information that comes from a reliable source. Today proving the trustworthiness of a source is of greater importance than ever before. Anyone can publish anything on the Internet without any basis in fact. When you want to use something that has been published, check the source to make sure they have fact checking and they have sourced their data and quotes. I place more trust in sources that adhere to publishing standards, such as respected educational institutions, refereed academic journals, and major news organizations. While this is not an absolute guarantee of truthfulness, it at least assures you that some verification has been done and your risk of the information being fictitious is reduced.

The second way to support a point is to quote an acknowledged expert. It could be a recognized internal subject matter expert in your organization, or it could be an industry expert who has a long history of being recognized by other organizations and publications. It may also be a research organization who produces reports and white papers on this area. As with published information, check the source and perhaps verify any quotes with a second source or the individual expert.

The third, and most common, support we use is the results of our own analysis. As with all of the sources of support, we need to make sure that the analysis does not contain errors. Perform spot checks of data that has been transcribed to make sure there are no errors. Check the formulas to make sure that the right components have been included and calculated properly. Do a reasonability test against other known data to see if these calculations fit a larger pattern. These checks and others that may be specific to your type of data are even more crucial when you are presenting something that is contrary to what has been accepted in the past.

When you deal with legal or regulatory topics, you may need to use the fourth way of supporting a point, which is by quoting legal or regulatory documents. As for published information, make sure you get these quotes from the source document, not a summary or paraphrase someone else published.

A fifth way to support a point is to provide a case study. Case studies are particularly useful when the point you are making is that a proposed solution will work in a situation that it has not previously been applied to. There is doubt as to whether the solution will work. The case study summarizes an application of a similar solution to a similar problem that resulted in a positive outcome. Because the problem and solution are similar to the present situation, the case study provides reassurance that there is a good chance of the solution providing a positive outcome in this situation.

Conclusion at the start or the end?

I am often asked whether presenters should save the conclusion for the end of their presentation or reveal it at the start of the presentation. I prefer to answer this based on hundreds of experiments done by the brain-science community as cited by John Medina is his book *Brain Rules*.

The result of these experiments all show that presenting ideas in a logically organized, hierarchical structure organized around core concepts results in typically a 40 percent improvement in remembering the ideas. I created the hierarchical structure of topics, points, and supporting information above so you will remember it better and use it to create more effective presentations.

Where does a hierarchical structure start? With the biggest idea, your conclusion. That is why I suggest starting your presentation with the conclusion you want the audience to remember when they leave. Don't save it for the end in a big reveal. Next explain the highest level of the structure, the topics, in an agenda. Then you can explain the points and supporting information in that structure.

You may be concerned that by presenting the conclusion first, the audience may not want to pay attention to the rest of the presentation or they may immediately start asking questions if they don't agree with the conclusion. I suggest that you can keep their attention by stating that the rest of the presentation will provide detailed support for the conclusion. By presenting the details in the proper context, the information will be clearer and you are happy to take questions and have a deeper discussion. Most people will want to hear the rest of your message so that they can come to their own conclusion and then discuss it with you.

CHAPTER SIX

Documenting the GPS for Presentations

Once you have decided on the Goal, Present Situation, and the Steps (including the topics, points, and supporting information) in your presentation, you should organize and document the plan. Why? Because documenting allows for review by yourself and others that will save hours of re-work later on.

Organizing the content

I usually suggest organizing the topics, points, and supporting information using sticky notes on a wall or desk. The topics are placed in a row across the top of the surface, then the points and supporting information organized under each topic in a hierarchical manner. Here is an example of an outline (different shapes have been used to make the levels in the outline easier to distinguish):

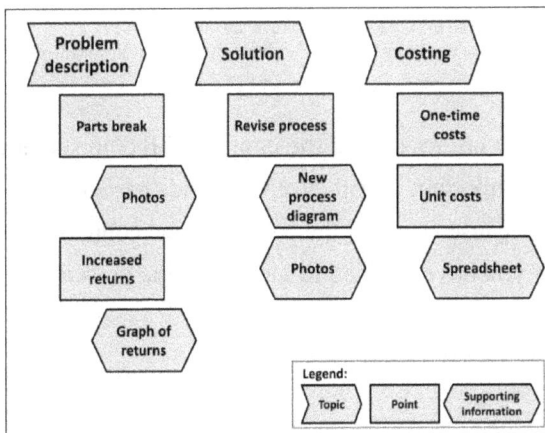

By organizing the content all in one place at first, you can see if there are gaps in the hierarchy or if the order needs to change for the flow to make sense to the audience.

Documenting the plan

I am often asked if organizing the content can be done electronically instead of using sticky notes. It can, and is part of the method I suggest for documenting the whole presentation plan. I suggest you use a landscape oriented Word document that has three pages, each serving a specific purpose.

The first page documents the Goal and Present Situation. Here is what the first page looks like for an example financial presentation.

Goal:

At the end of the presentation the Management Team will have the information they need to make decisions on spending for next quarter to meet annual profit goals.

Present Situation:

- Have heads of departments in room
- Concerns about expense levels with revenue under pressure
- Need to make details available for further study afterwards by staff in each area

When you are reviewing the content of the presentation with others, it is important that they understand the Goal and Present Situation, because it gives them the proper context to evaluate the content you have decided to include in the presentation.

The second page captures the organized content in a table format.

Revenue	Op Ex	Cap Ex	Forecast
Comparison to projections • Graph of projection vs. actual for each product line Trend YTD • Total revenue trend as line graph	Largest variances from budget • Table of top % variances • Table of top $ variances Suggested actions • List of actions to consider	Scope progress vs. expectation • Gantt chart of actual vs. expected progress Budget analysis • Bar charts of a) variance actual vs. expected for completed scope, b) variance projected vs. budget	EBITDA forecast • Table of current vs. previous forecast with variance Areas of emphasis for Q4 • Actions and who is responsible

The table has as many columns as you have topics (usually no more than five). The table has two rows. The topics are entered in the first row, one per column. In the second row, enter the points and supporting information for each point, using an indent to indicate the supporting information under each point. In the above example I have used a bullet point for the supporting information to make it easier to visually distinguish. Notice that by adding more detail to the supporting information in the plan, it will make it easier for others to know exactly what you are considering, and it will make the creation of the slides easier later on, since you know exactly what needs to be created.

The third page captures the additional content that you will have available for the audience that is not being shown during the presentation. In the next chapter I will explain what goes into each of the three sections of this page, the Before, After, and Behind sections.

Before:
- Link to financial statements on intranet
-

After:
- Link to presentation in PDF with backup slides unhidden
-

Behind:
- Hidden slide with breakdown of sales by region
- Hyperlink to Revenue projection model if assumptions challenged
- Hidden slide of reasons for delays on CapEx projects
-

Reviewing the plan

Once you have documented the plan in the above manner, it becomes easy to review it with others. Since it is in Word format, you can send it to others and ask them to use the Track Changes feature of Word that allows them to indicate what changes they suggest be made. When the document is sent back to you, the changes are marked and you can accept or reject each one. If you accept the change, it automatically updates the document.

If you are working in a real-time collaborative environment where everyone can make changes to the document online, you can have a meeting where everyone is editing the document at the same time with changes reflected real-time on each person's screen. This can cut down on the delays waiting for emails to be returned, and can allow everyone to build on each other's ideas in real time.

Reviewing the plan in Word format is much better than the usual method of creating slides and sending the PowerPoint file for review by email. The typical review process I see in organizations ends up creating many versions of a PowerPoint file. This review method takes a lot of time and is often not effective.

There are two key problems that I observe in the typical review of slides. First, when you have spent 45 minutes creating what you consider to be a great slide and someone else draws a big red "X" through it, it hurts. That hurt often translates into trying to justify the slide because you have so much time invested in it. With a Word document, there is not the time investment, so changes can be looked at more objectively.

The second problem is that PowerPoint does not allow you to look at the entire presentation in a hierarchical manner. It becomes hard to do a complete review of the key messages, especially if the slides are not clear. The result is far more rounds of reviews, resulting in dozens of versions of the presentation. When I look at all the versions, I find that at least the first 50% are just trying to get the messages figured out. By using a clear structure in Word, you eliminate a lot of the review time because the focus is only on the messages, not trying to figure out the structure of the content from unclear slides.

CHAPTER SEVEN

Focusing the content

The biggest issue in presentations today is information overload. Respondents to my audience survey say this, and I hear it from almost every prospect who contacts me about my workshops. Overwhelming the audience with content has almost become an epidemic in presentations. Once you have created the plan for your presentation, go back through the content you have planned and look for ways to focus the information on just what the audience needs to hear. The last page of the document in the previous chapter gets completed as you use the techniques in this chapter to reduce the content you show the audience.

The goal is to get the audience over the hurdle

When we use a GPS system to take a journey, does it show us every street we are going to pass? No. It selects the right level of information that will help us successfully make the trip. We need to do the same in our presentations. We need to select the right level of detail for the audience. Let me share an analogy that will help to explain the different levels of detail and where we want to aim in our presentations.

The analogy I want to use is the Olympic event called the decathlon. In the decathlon the athletes compete in ten different athletic events accumulating points for their performance in each of those events. At the end they add up all the points and the person with the highest number of points gets the gold medal.

In the decathlon there are three events where they have to jump over something. The first event is the hurdles. A standard hurdle in athletics is 42 inches high. How do they get over each hurdle? They have trained so that they can run full speed at the hurdle, leap up over it, land, and keep running full speed toward the next hurdle.

The second event where they have to jump over something is the high jump. To get 900 points or more, which is a very good score in a decathlon event, you have to jump 83 inches or higher. Do they use the same technique in the high jump as they did in the hurdles? No, not at all. They don't even run at it from the front. They come at it from the side and then they turn and arch their back and leap up over the bar. They use a totally different technique because it is a totally different event.

The third event that they have to jump over something is the pole vault. To get 900 points or more, you have to pole vault over 195 inches. Do they use a technique for the pole vault that they used in either of the other two events? No, not at all. They have a very long pole. They run at full-speed, plant the pole in this tiny hole in the ground, flex the pole, whip themselves up over the bar and hope to land on the padded surface on the other side. They use a totally different technique because it is a totally different event.

Here is how this applies to presentations. I believe the event we are competing in is simply getting our audience over the hurdle of understanding. That is all we need to do. Unfortunately, some presenters believe that they are in the high jump and this requires them to include in their presentation the answer to every possible question the audience might ask. This is a different technique because it is a different event, unfortunately not the event we are competing in. And some presenters believe they are in the pole vault so they not only present the answers to all possible questions, they also include all the data, calculations, formulas, inputs, and anything else that might be slightly related. Again, this is the wrong technique because the presenter thinks they are competing in a different event, the pole vault, than the event we are really competing in, the hurdles. If our event is the hurdles, please don't pole vault over a hurdle – it will likely be painful if you attempt it.

In my workshops I show an example of a pole vault slide. It is a spreadsheet covering most of the slide with a rounded rectangle in the lower left corner that states the conclusion. There are over 390 numbers on the slide, some with six decimal places, but only the one in the lower left box is relevant. All the rest are the calculations used to come to the conclusion. The audience likely won't even see that one relevant number because they are overwhelmed with the rest of the slide.

The slide I show isn't close to the record I have seen for largest number of cells from an Excel spreadsheet copied onto a single slide. The top two that I have seen had 1,975 cells and 2,100 cells! I can't make that up. The question you are probably asking yourself is, "Why would anybody ever do that?!?" Both of these slides were submitted to me as part of sample presentations, so I got to ask the person in the room why they used a slide that clearly no one would be able to read. In both cases, I got the exact same answer, "To show how much work we did!" They thought they were competing in the pole vault so felt compelled to include every detail of the calculations.

Spreadsheets on slides also cause a big problem because you invite the audience to go hunting for questions in the numbers.

You have probably seen this happen in a presentation. A spreadsheet is displayed and someone picks out a number in a corner of the spreadsheet that is totally irrelevant to what you wanted to talk about. Then they become like a dog on a bone on that number, driving deeper and deeper with questions on it. Twenty minutes later you realize your presentation is totally off track because you've gone down this path of answering questions about a number that isn't relevant to the message. The reality is, we invited that sidetracking by putting the spreadsheet of numbers on the slide.

The quality of the conclusion matters more than the quantity of work

Another reason I see spreadsheets on slides is that the presenter thinks that the executives want to see how much effort went into the analysis. The presenter did a lot of work and wants to show it. If they only showed a few numbers on the slide, how would the executives know that the analysis was thorough and well done?

When the executives see the spreadsheet on the screen, they get overwhelmed by all the numbers. They may get confused. They may ask to just "give me the bottom line" or something similar. If they are detail oriented, the executive may ask questions about one inconsequential number that has nothing to do with the real message.

None of these reactions are what the presenter thought they would get. The presenter thought the executives would be so impressed with the volume of work that was done. The problem is that the executives care more about the quality of the conclusion than the quantity of work that was done. The executive role is about making important decisions to move the organization forward towards the goals that have been set. This requires insight from analysis of data and situations.

The executives hire competent professionals to do the analysis. Ones who have the experience and education to understand and analyze the data. If the professional isn't qualified, they won't get the job. What the executive is looking for is an insightful conclusion from the analysis. They will judge the professional by the quality of the conclusion. Is it uncovering new insights? Is it giving them information that they haven't seen before? Is the conclusion going to give them an advantage over the competition in the marketplace?

If the analysis has been done well, it will show in the conclusion. Most executives frankly don't care how many spreadsheet cells were filled in or how many hours were spent. They hire talented professionals to do the analysis and present insightful conclusions. They don't want to have to figure out the conclusion from a spreadsheet on a slide.

Spreadsheets are for calculation, not communication

I agree that Excel is an excellent tool for analyzing data. But I want presenters to remember that spreadsheets were designed for calculations, they were not designed as a communication tool. When I suggest this in some workshops, I get the response from a participant that their boss requires the spreadsheet to be on the slide. It is important to understand why this request might happen and what you can do about it.

The first question you should ask when your boss requests the full spreadsheet on the slide is why they want to see the full spreadsheet. They are clearly looking for something, and it will save you a lot of time if you know what they are looking for. If they really only need to see the bottom line, just show them a clean visual or small table with the key figures. This is almost never the case unfortunately, so why else might they want to see so many numbers?

The least likely answer is that they don't trust your work and they need to see all the calculations that went into the result. If they have an issue with your work, they will address it in a performance discussion, not a slide request.

A reason I hear frequently is that the slides are being used as documentation for either archives or as part of a contract, so all the details need to be there. While some commenters would suggest creating a separate document, I know you don't have the time to do that. Create slides that highlight the key points using visuals to communicate the message, then include the detailed spreadsheets as hidden slides in the file. That way, the details are there, but not seen in Slide Show mode. We will talk more about moving content before, after, or behind the presentation later in this chapter.

Another common reason is that the boss wants the details there in case someone has a question. What they don't realize is that putting all the details on the screen actually invites unrelated questions as people scour the spreadsheet finding areas they want to ask about. These areas are often unrelated to the message you want to communicate and derail the presentation. Again, put the details on hidden slides and add hyperlinks from your visual presentation slides to jump to the hidden detail slides if someone does have a relevant question.

In my experience the most common reason the boss asks for the entire spreadsheet on the slide is because they aren't getting what they need in most presentations. Leaders need actionable insights on what needs to be done next. Insights that consider the context of the results, the relationships between the data and other factors. They are almost always only getting measurement results that answer what happened or performance results that answer how the results compare to a previous period or goal. They ask for the spreadsheet so they can figure out the insights themselves. If you provide them the insights they need, they won't ask for the spreadsheet.

Make the details available Before, After, or Behind the presentation

When I suggest presenters remove spreadsheets or paragraphs of text from their slides, the most common objection is that the audience won't ever know those details, which may be important to them at some point in time. Many presenters think they only have one opportunity to share information with the audience, in the presentation. So they put everything in the presentation, afraid of leaving anything out.

This is another area where looking at what a GPS system does can help guide our approach. The GPS doesn't show you every detail of every building on every road you are travelling on. What it does is allow you to access more details before, after, or behind what it shows you.

Before you start your trip, it allows you to explore more about the route you will be following, such as stops along the way, interesting side trips, or road issues that may impact your trip. During the trip, it allows you to access more details using pinch to zoom. You can zoom in to see more details of the streets and buildings as you go along if you need to, but only if you need to. At the end of the trip, the GPS system offers to show you more details about the destination, such as nearby restaurants, hotels, or attractions.

We apply this same idea to the information in our presentations. Instead of putting all the details into the presentation, we decide which details could go before, after, or behind our presentation. Let's look at each of these options in more detail.

Before the presentation

The before opportunity is information we make available to the audience in advance of the presentation. This is often called a pre-read. The purpose is to give the audience all the details, the analysis, and the background so that they can review and consider them. This gives them the context so they come prepared for the discussion and the decisions that need to be made in the meeting.

The big mistake presenters make when using a pre-read is that they send their presentation as the pre-read. If you do this, don't be surprised if early on in your presentation an executive interrupts and says, "Why are you presenting this? I've already read this. Why are you wasting my time?" If all you do is read the pre-read, you are not needed, they can read on their own. In the presentation we should just focus on the key points that we need them to understand, the discussions of the information, and the decisions that need to be made. The pre-read prepares them with the details.

After the presentation

The after opportunity is often referred to as supplemental information. It used to be mailed out after the presentation but now we just send a link to the documents on a server. It allows the audience members to dive deeper into an area if they want to. Access to the details may also be required due to legal or regulatory reasons. We make it available, and the audience members make the decision whether to review it or not.

Behind the slides for the presentation

The behind opportunity is the one that most presenters will gravitate towards initially because it allows you to access detailed information during the presentation if a question is asked. Most presenters want the comfort that the details are accessible and they won't be left looking unprepared if a question is asked.

There are two options for accessing detailed information: source files or hidden slides. In both cases, you create a hyperlink from an object on the slide to the details you want to access. If a question gets asked that requires you to show the details, you use the hyperlink to jump to the details.

Source files would be the best choice when the question may require recalculating some results or accessing a certain page in a long document. In those situations, the hyperlink opens the source file on top of the presentation, allowing the presenter to scroll to the appropriate spot and even make changes if needed. Because the program, such as Excel or Word, is open on top of the presentation, all the features are available to the presenter. You can save and close the file, which will return you to the presentation where you were before you activated the hyperlink.

Think of accessing source files like accessing more details on a GPS where the system accesses the information from the server in real time. Linking to a source file requires access to that file location during the presentation.

If all you need to show are some additional details in a table or text, a hidden slide would be the best choice. A hidden slide is a slide that is in your PowerPoint file but it will not show up in Slide Show mode unless you specifically request it. These hidden slides can be included or excluded when printing the slides or saving them as a PDF file using the options in these features. After you have displayed the hidden slide, you can return to the slide you were on to continue the presentation. Hidden slides are like offline maps for a GPS system. In offline mode a GPS can use the details it has stored, but can't access updated information, such as current traffic. A hidden slide contains the information you put on it, but any real-time or updated information will not be accessible.

Hyperlink to the details removed from the slides

The method you use to access either a source file or a hidden slide in PowerPoint is to use a hyperlink. A hyperlink can be added to any object on a slide: an image, a shape, text, a graph, etc. When adding the hyperlink, you can choose the destination, either a file/web address or a slide in the current presentation. If you choose a slide, you can identify the hidden slides because the slide number will have round brackets around it.

To use the hyperlink during the presentation, you have two options. The first option is use the mouse and click on the hyperlinked object. This requires you to be close enough to the computer to use the mouse or trackpad, or it requires you to use a presentation remote that has full mouse capabilities. I don't prefer this method because I find the pointer movement on the screen distracting.

The second option for using a hyperlink on a slide is the keyboard method. In Slide Show mode, pressing the Tab key will place a thin white and black dashed box around the hyperlinked object. If you have more than one hyperlinked object, you can press the Tab key again to move to the next object. To activate the hyperlink, press the Enter key.

When you are using hidden slides you can also access them even if you don't have a hyperlinked object on that slide. In Slide Show mode, press Ctrl+S (hold the Ctrl key and press the S key). This will display a list of all slides in your file on the screen. The hidden slides will have round brackets around the slide numbers. Use your arrow keys or mouse to select the slide you want displayed. To return to the previous slide, press Ctrl+S again and look at the bottom of the list to see Last Slide Viewed. This is the slide you need to return to in order to continue the presentation.

You can also display any slide by typing the slide number on the keyboard and pressing Enter. This technique is good to use if you want to use backup slides in an Appendix section at the end of your file. You will need to have a list of slide numbers that you may need to access if questions are asked so that you can quickly jump to the appropriate slide using this technique.

If you are concerned that audience members will ask to see every hidden slide or source file if they see hyperlinked objects on the screen or hyperlinked text, consider hiding the hyperlinks in invisible objects. Draw a shape, add a hyperlink to it, test that the link works, then set the fill and outline colors of the shape to No Color. This makes the shape invisible and will not draw the attention of the audience. You will probably want to use the keyboard method to activate the hyperlink as it can be difficult to use the mouse to click on an object you can't see on the slide.

The audience doesn't need all the details

When I explain how presenters can move details off their slides into hidden slides or source files and access the details using hyperlinks, I hear one common concern. Presenters are convinced that the audience really wants all the details and they will be accessing 85% or more of the hyperlinked details during the presentation.

Instead of me trying to convince you again that the audience doesn't really need all the details, let me share what one participant told me in a workshop in Ludwigshafen, Germany. She had been taught to use hidden slides by some of her colleagues in Chicago I had trained previously. She was convinced that the audience would ask for almost every detail she had taken off her slides. She shared that her actual experience was that she used less than 20% of the links. The audience doesn't need to see the details if you share a clear message that shows insight and you make those details accessible before, after, or behind the presentation.

CHAPTER EIGHT

Visually displaying one step at a time

After your journey is planned, the GPS system gives you step-by-step instructions so that you successfully follow the best route and arrive at your destination. The GPS system uses a specific approach that we can apply to creating the visuals for our presentations.

Three elements of the display

When the GPS system starts to display each step to us, it uses a specific technique. At the top of the screen, it summarizes that step in text, such as "Head southwest on I-190 W" It also shows us a relevant section of the map with a line to indicate the route we are to follow. Finally, it adds an indicator, usually some form of an arrow, to indicate where we are on the map and what direction we need to head so that we can focus our attention on the action we need to take at that time.

This is a good model for us to follow when thinking about creating slides for our presentation. I suggest each slide have a headline at the top that summarizes the key message of the slide. The majority of the rest of the slide contains a visual that illustrates the message, perhaps a graph, diagram, photo, or list of text points for context. Finally, we focus the attention of the audience on the slide content through the use of callouts or builds on the slide.

My book *Select Effective Visuals* goes into detail on all three of these steps in creating an effective slide, so I will just provide a brief overview here.

The headline summarizes the message you want the audience to understand from your slide. If you skip this step, it will be very hard to select an effective visual because you won't know what the visual is supposed to communicate. The best way to get clear on your message is to write it as a summary sentence, like newspapers do at the top of every story.

Selecting the right visual for a slide is the one step many business professionals find the most challenging. In *Select Effective Visuals* I suggest that almost every message a business presentation needs to communicate can be organized into one of six categories. I break those categories down into 30 groups and sub-groups and show 66 individual visuals that presenters should consider using. The following table shows some of the most common messages and some of the visuals you should consider using to illustrate that message on your slides.

Message	Possible visuals
Comparing values to a single standard	Column, bar, or line graph with a dashed line showing the standard
Comparing values in a single data series	Column graph or bar chart Proportional object collection (if values are an order of magnitude different) Grouped item comparison or ISOTYPE diagram

Comparing values in two or more data series	Multiple width overlapping column graph
	Small multiples column or bar graphs
Comparing one component to the whole or total	Pie chart
	Donut graph
	Multiple 100% stacked bars
Showing components that explain the difference between a starting value and an ending value	Waterfall graph
	Steps to a total graph
Showing a trend in one or more data series	Line graph
Linear sequence of steps	Chevron diagram
	Shapes on an arrow
	Decision tree
Time based information	Gantt chart
	Timeline
Related points	Text points/Bullet points
Comparison	Table
A person, place or object	Images with explanatory text
Example or demonstration	Highlighted text in a quote
	Case study
	Audio or video clip

Focusing the audience is done when you deliver the presentation, but you must plan this when you create each slide. You can add callouts to direct the audience's attention to one part of the visual, whether it is a graph, diagram, or image. You can also use the animation feature of PowerPoint to build the content of the slide piece by piece so that you can give the audience the correct context before they come to a conclusion.

By creating our slides using the same approach that a GPS uses to display each step along the trip, we can effectively communicate each message visually.

Headline template for the results of analysis

To help you write effective headlines for your slides, let me share a template that can be used when presenting a conclusion or result of analysis that has been performed. This is a common situation many business presenters find themselves in. The temptation is to state the topic of the analysis as the headline. This does not give the audience the conclusion that tells them what they need to know about the analysis.

Instead, the headline should contain the two key components the audience needs to see: the area that was analyzed and the conclusion. The first key component is stating what area, item, data, issue, etc. you were analyzing. This part is important because you have to make sure that the audience has the context for understanding the importance of the conclusion.

The second key part states the conclusion or result of your analysis. I believe it is important to state the conclusion up front at the top of the slide so the audience knows where you are going as you explain the details of the analysis when you discuss the rest of the slide.

Arrange the key parts in the order that makes sense, including a verb between the two if necessary. The verb is usually a simple connecting verb such as "shows" or a form of the verb "to be".

The template has two options for structuring the headline. The first option is to use the structure <Analyzed area> <Verb> <Conclusion>. An example would be, "Average transaction amount is consistent across regions" This headline tells the audience the result of the analysis in a clear, concise manner.

The second option is to reverse the two key components, using <Conclusion> <Verb> <Analyzed area>. An example would be "Michigan, Florida, and Maryland are top states for fraud loss" Again the key point is clear in the headline.

While this template applies to presenting the results of analysis, I hope it shows you how important a clear, concise headline is for your slides. Please do not skip this step in creating each slide, as it is crucial for selecting the right visual and it makes the message of each slide clear to the audience.

The number of slides doesn't matter

When a GPS system presents the steps to you, it does so one step at a time. If it showed you four or five steps at once, you would be confused and likely not make the correct turns or take the correct roads. It is the same when presenting each message to the audience in our presentation. We should present one message at a time, one message per slide. When I state this in my workshops many presenters get concerned because they realize that this will result in more slides in their presentation.

Why are more slides a concern? Because I know what almost every business professional does when they receive a PowerPoint file in their Inbox. They open up the attachment and immediately look at the lower left corner of the PowerPoint window to see how many slides are in the file. Each person has a number in mind that they consider to be the "correct" number of slides that should be in a presentation. If the number of slides in the file is greater than the "correct" number, they have instantly judged this presentation to be not worthy. Please stop judging presentations based on the number of slides, it has nothing to do with the effectiveness of the presentation.

Would you refuse to use a GPS system to take a trip simply because it gives you more than a certain number of steps or turns? That sounds crazy, and it is. But for some reason many business professionals do this when it comes to the number of slides in a PowerPoint file.

An audience in a live presentation or an executive who is emailed a PowerPoint file can better understand one clear message per slide compared to fewer slides that are crowded and confusing. If they are reviewing an emailed file, they can actually review it faster if the slides have a single clear message because they can glance at the slide, absorb the important point, and move on to the next slide. They don't have to spend time trying to figure out the message from the overload of text, numbers, and visuals on each slide.

In almost every workshop I deliver, we have to discuss the request from executives to limit the number of slides their staff uses in a presentation. The executives commonly ask that no more than five slides be used when presenting to the management team. Even after they have made this request, the executives don't see more effective presentations. In fact, they often see worse presentations.

Let's first look at why executives make this request for five slides. It could be five, four, or any small number, the reasoning behind it is the same. Executives have seen far too many presentations that are data dumps. The presenter spews forth information that overwhelms the executives. The problem is the executives don't get the key insights they are looking for. They need to solve this problem with staff presentations because it is a waste of their time, it delays decision making, and it takes a huge amount of time for the staff to create these presentations.

The executives figure that if they limit the staff to only a few slides, the staff will narrow down all the information and present only those key insights that the executives need to know. Then they will get focused, action oriented presentations from their staff that enables the executives to make decisions. Sounds like a perfect solution.

Except the staff don't understand why the slide limit is being imposed. They don't know what is wrong with their current presentations. They figure it is just a way to reduce the time presentations take, or a paper reduction effort when presentations are printed. So the staff spend time figuring out how to cram twenty slides worth of information onto five slides. They drop the font size down into single digit point sizes. They resize graphs so that they are impossible to see. And they squish diagrams and images into tiny spaces on the slide.

In the mind of the staff, they have done exactly what the executives want. They have reduced the number of slides down to five. When the executives see these presentations, they are frustrated, as they should be. These presentations are even worse, because now they can't possibly read anything on the slides. The request backfired because the executives made the wrong request.

Instead of placing a limit of the number of slides, the executives should request a maximum of five actions or insights based on the staff's analysis of the situation. Each action or insight would be backed up by a few key facts and tie to one of the organization's overall goals for the year. It could be that they should stay the course in an area that is performing well. It could be that corrective action needs to be taken on an issue that has been identified. It could be that a risk should be mitigated before it causes an issue. Or any number of other actions that the staff has identified that will help the organization reach its goals.

To create these actions and insights, the staff has to go beyond the typical data dump. They have to consider the data in the context of the overall situation, look at interactions between areas, and consider how the action will help a goal be reached. The presentation is no longer focused on the data, but what the data means to the organization. That is what the executives really need to know.

This may fit into five slides but it may need more than five slides. If you get asked to limit the slides in a presentation you are creating, use the techniques in the previous chapters to focus on the few insights that the executives need to know about and the actions your analysis suggest needs to be taken. Then create one message per slide. The number of slides doesn't matter, the clarity of your message is what is important.

Separate thinking from mechanics

When creating slides, don't start in PowerPoint. Too often presenters sit down at their computer to start creating their slides. I suggest you start planning the headline, visual, and focus techniques on paper first so you can separate the thinking about the slides from the mechanics of creating them.

When you start in the software, you see the default instruction from PowerPoint to "Click to add text" Even if you want to go beyond just using text, you start to explore the other options in the program and get lost discovering new options instead of focusing on the message you want to communicate. The mechanics of creating the slides can wait until later.

Start by planning your slides on paper first. Start by writing the headline using the ideas above. Select the visual that will communicate the message and sketch it out so you know what you want to create when it comes time to work in the software. Note where the data or source of the information is so you can easily access it when needed. Finally, write down how you will focus the audience during the delivery of the slide.

Once you have planned each slide on paper, the mechanics of creating the slides is much easier. You don't waste time exploring the software options. You can be focused and quickly create the slides. Past participants in my workshops tell me that they save over 50% of the time they used to spend creating slides by planning them on paper first.

The clearest example of the separation between thinking and mechanics is a large strategy consulting firm. None of their consultants ever create their own slides anymore. What they do is sketch their slides either on paper or their tablet and assemble the sketches into a PDF file. The file is sent to a service in India overnight. The people there create all the slides in the company template, and email it so when the consultant wakes up in Europe or North America, their slides are in their email Inbox.

I don't share this with you to suggest you should use such a service. The reason I share it is because it is a clear distinction between the value of thinking and of mechanics. They have very clearly defined the high value work, the thinking, and that's what they want their consultants to do. The lower value work, the mechanics, that's what they outsource. You can do the same even if you don't use this outsourcing approach. Spend more of your time on the thinking, the high value work, so you can reduce the amount of time you spend on the mechanics, the lower value work.

You don't always need a slide on the screen

There is no rule saying you always have to have a slide on the screen. When you want to focus the audience and not distract them with a visual on the screen, use a planned or spontaneous black slide. Your presentation will be more effective when you do.

The basic premise of a black slide is that there is nothing on the screen for the audience to look at. In the absence of a visual, where does the audience naturally look? At the presenter. Now, as the presenter, you have 100% of the audience's attention. Nothing is distracting them from what you are about to say. That is quite powerful. So when should you use a black slide?

The first use is when you want the audience's complete attention on what you are about to share, such as telling a powerful story that illustrates your point. In my workshops, I demonstrate this use when I black the screen and tell a story about how the idea I have just shared with the participants helped in a real presentation situation. The audience is paying full attention to you when you tell the story.

In this first use of a black slide, you know exactly when the story will be told and you can create a black slide in your PowerPoint file. The easiest way to create a black slide is to add a new slide and draw a black rectangle to cover up the entire slide. This method is much easier than trying to change the background of the slide to black. It also will work when you copy this slide to another place in your presentation or even another presentation.

The second use for a black slide is not something you can plan for in advance. When someone asks a question during the presentation, should you leave the slide up or go to a black slide? The answer depends on whether the visual on the screen is relevant to the answer you are giving. If the visual is not related to the answer, go to a black slide. That way, the audience will focus only on the answer you are giving and not be distracted or confused by the visual that does not relate to the answer. How can you go to a black slide at any time during your presentation? Simply press the period key (.) in Slide Show mode in PowerPoint. Press the period key again to return to your last slide. The period key acts as a toggle to turn the display of the current slide off and on.

The third use for a black slide could be planned or could be spontaneous. Any time you want to move in the room and will walk through the beam of the projector, go to a black slide before you move. One of the most annoying things you can do is walk through the projected image or stand blocking part of it. If you want to move from one side of the room to the other, just go to a black slide, move across the room, then go back to the slide you want to speak about. If this is planned as part of your presentation, you can create a black slide at that spot in the presentation using the technique described above. If it is spontaneous, black out the slide using the period key described above.

Using the period key to black out the slide does not have to tie you to your laptop. Almost every presentation remote has a button that will black the screen. Since the remote is seen as a keyboard by the computer, it is really pressing the key on the keyboard when you click the button on the remote.

Delivering a presentation over the web is the one situation that using a black slide will not work. The methods above will technically work on a web meeting system. The problem is that the remote audience will think the black screen indicates the connection has been lost. They will lose focus and ask about the apparent connection issues, or they will disconnect and reconnect, missing part of your presentation. This is why in a previous chapter I suggested you consider the logistics of each presentation as you prepare the message and how you will best deliver it.

Focus the words in each point

In the list of possible visuals earlier in this chapter you may have been surprised to see that text points or bullet points was included as a visual. I think text points play an important role in giving our audience context for related items we want to discuss.

That is why I think a bullet point or text point slide will continue to be an important visual in many presentations.

When you are writing text or bullet points, resist the temptation to add more words than are absolutely necessary to get your point across. This is difficult, because a text point should not be a full sentence, which is what we are familiar with writing. If we want to visually declutter text slides, we need to reduce the words on each slide.

To reduce the words in each text point and get your point across clearly, I use eight strategies to remove words and phrases from text points. Each strategy may or may not apply in every situation. Below are the strategies and then I show three examples of the strategies being applied to actual text points from client slides.

Strategy #1: Cut any phrases that are extra detail to the one key message you are trying to communicate in this point. We are experts in the area and we have a natural tendency to want to share everything we know. It hurts, but we need to cut the extra detail from our text points so only the key message remains.

Strategy #2: Remove most extra words such as "the", "that", and "a." Yes, this will not make the point a proper sentence, but we don't want it to be. These extra words don't make the message clearer for the audience.

Strategy #3: Remove most forms of the verb "to be", such as "is", "was", etc. When you don't have to create a grammatically correct sentence, you can remove these verbs that don't add meaning to a point.

Strategy #4: Don't repeat text that is in the slide headline. Once the headline has established the message of the slide, we don't need to repeat what area we are talking about in a text point. Assume the audience knows the area from the headline. Since each slide has only one message, all of the points on the slide relate to that one area.

Strategy #5: Where possible, switch from passive verb forms to an active verb or noun form. This makes each point much stronger and more direct. The clearer each point is, the more likely the audience will understand your message.

Strategy #6: Replace direction words with a symbol (↑ or ▲ instead of up/increase; ↓ or ▼ instead of down/decrease). These symbols are visual indicators to the audience that allow them to quickly interpret the meaning. Often these symbols are used before numbers in a text point.

Strategy #7: Replace words like "because" or "due to" with a colon (:). Again, this strategy is aimed at making points clearer by replacing words with a visual, in this case a punctuation character.

Strategy #8: Change fancy words to simpler words. In some industries and areas, presenters think that if they use long, fancy sounding words, the audience will think they are more qualified on the topic. The risk is that the audience may not know what the word means or they may think the presenter is trying to hide or confuse an issue. Stick instead with words you commonly use when speaking.

Example #1

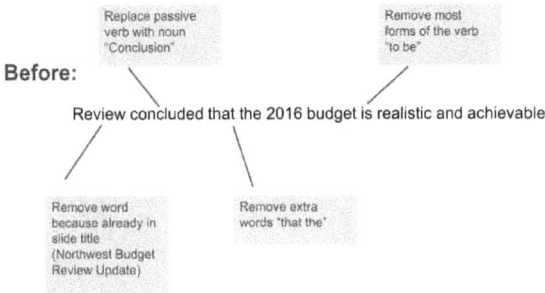

Before:

Review concluded that the 2016 budget is realistic and achievable

After:

Conclusion: 2016 budget realistic and achievable

Example #2

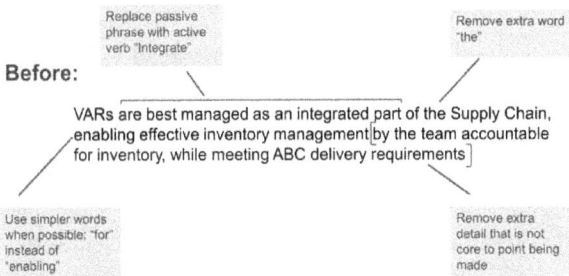

Before:

VARs are best managed as an integrated part of the Supply Chain, enabling effective inventory management by the team accountable for inventory, while meeting ABC delivery requirements

After:

Integrate VARs in Supply Chain for effective inventory management

Example #3

Replace directional
word with symbol

Before:

Out of stock items were reduced by 8.7% as a result of the
implementation of the new inventory system

Remove words that
are not necessary

Replace "because",
"as a result of", or
"due to" with a
colon (:)

After:

New inventory system: out of stock items ↓ 8.7%

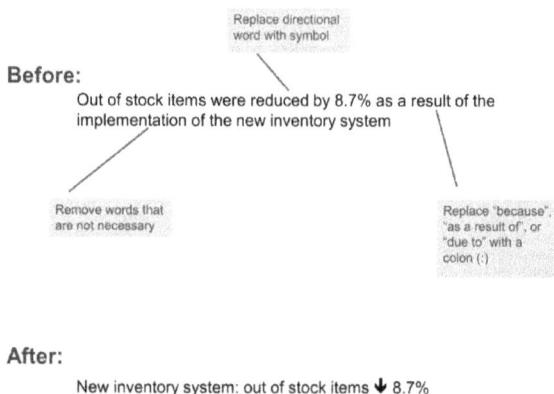

Present actionable insights from analysis

Earlier I suggested using visuals instead of spreadsheets when presenting numbers and listed examples of some visuals you should consider. Many of the visuals allow you to more clearly show the results of analysis.

In my book *Select Effective Visuals*, I discuss the three different types of results you can present when discussing analysis. The first is measurement results, which answer the question, "What did we do?" Sometimes referred to as data, it is meaningless on its own, so we rarely present this type of result. Most of the time presenters offer performance results, which answer the question, "How did we do?" The data is put into a spreadsheet and compared to the goal, previous time period, industry average, or another relevant measure that will answer the question. These results are often displayed as spreadsheets on slides for the reasons discussed earlier.

What our audiences want is the third type of result, actionable insights, which answer the question, "What do we do next?" This is a question that can't be answered by simply displaying a spreadsheet. It requires the presenter to consider the context, the history, related areas, and other factors to conclude what actions should be taken based on the analysis. This is what our audiences really need.

It is common to have multiple insights from analyzing a situation. In this case, use multiple slides with one insight on each. Just like the GPS will display multiple steps in a small geographical area, presenters should display one insight at a time from the analysis so the audience can clearly understand each one. The visual may be different for each insight, depending on the message you want to deliver.

There are situations when you will want to use a single visual to communicate more than one insight because the insights all come from the one visual. In this case, use callouts that are built on the slide one at a time so that you can focus the audience on one part of the visual for each insight.

CHAPTER NINE

Presenting like a GPS

When you are delivering your presentation, you can take some tips from the way a GPS system works.

Practice and Rehearse

A GPS system, like almost all software, is never finished. The developers are always looking for ways to improve the software based on user feedback. As presenters, we should be working to make our presentations better through two key ways to get feedback on a presentation: practice and rehearsal.

Practice and rehearsal are two different activities. Practice is running through your presentation silently, in your mind. You may advance through your slides, thinking through what you plan to say; check you have the right speaking notes, and become more comfortable with the sequence of the points. Practice is important, but it is not sufficient.

You also need to rehearse, which is standing and delivering your presentation out loud, as if you are in front of the audience. Rehearsing is the only way to make sure what you planned to say comes out properly and flows well. It also allows you to make sure that your presentation will fit into the time allotted to you. If you can rehearse in the room you will be delivering in, you can also become familiar with the equipment you will be using. Both practice and rehearsal help prepare you to confidently deliver your presentation.

Test your slides

A GPS system goes through extensive testing to make sure that each step and each visual is accurate. The developers use a checklist to make sure they don't miss anything. As part of your preparation to present, you should test your slides. Here are some items to check during your tests.

Spelling and grammar

Unfortunately I see spelling errors on slides often. What does your audience think when they see spelling or grammatical errors? It is likely that your credibility will take a hit. A good way to catch these mistakes is to read the words on your slide in reverse order. By reading in reverse order, your brain won't anticipate the next word and skip over it even if it is misspelled (our brains anticipate the next word and assume it is correct if enough of the letters are in the correct spots).

Text wrapping

Sometimes text doesn't fit into a shape and one letter wraps onto the next line. This distracts the audience from your message. If you can't make the shape bigger, adjust the internal margin of the text within the shape. This internal margin adjustment is usually all that is needed for that last letter to join the rest of the word.

Animation sequence

This is something that you should test during your practice sessions. Carefully advance through each slide in Slide Show mode and focus on the sequence of builds to ensure they tell the story properly.

Contrast of Colors

When you place text on a colored background in a diagram or graph, make sure you have tested to see if the colors have enough contrast when projected (bright laptop screens can be deceiving because projectors don't show colors as brightly). Make sure you have tested your colors using the Color Contrast Calculator (at www.colorcontrastcalculator.com), and you test your slides on a projector, if possible, in the room you will be speaking in.

Broken or Misdirected Hyperlinks

When using the hyperlinks to hidden slides or source files discussed earlier, you should test that the hyperlinks go where you expect them to go. This is especially important for presentations that get updated with new slides or source files that change each month.

Manage audience expectations

Imagine if you were handed a GPS system and told to follow the directions it gives you but you weren't told the destination or the route in advance. Would you be anxious and have questions? I think the majority of us would.

The same reaction happens when the presenter doesn't tell the audience where they are going and how they will get there. Without a clear goal and an agenda of steps along the journey (the topics from the Steps in the GPS approach), the audience is unsure if they want to take this journey to an unknown destination. Their response? Ask questions. In the case of executives, they won't wait to find out if the presenter will give them the information they need, they interrupt with questions early in the presentation.

By stating a goal and giving an agenda at the start of the presentation, you let the audience know what is coming up. They now have context for what will come and they know that their topic will be addressed during the presentation. The anxiety is reduced because it is no longer an unknown journey. You have managed their expectations and they can relax and listen to the message you want to deliver.

This won't prevent all questions or interruptions, but it provides you with an opportunity to give the audience an overview of the route and the destination, just like a GPS does at the start of your trip.

Deliver each slide confidently

When a GPS system gives you verbal instructions, it does so confidently. It doesn't say, "I am thinking that perhaps you should consider turning left at the next intersection if you think that is a good idea." No, it confidently says, "In 200 feet, turn left onto Route 62." Similarly, you can deliver your slides with confidence knowing you have planned your message with the GPS approach and designed slides with one message per slide (containing a headline and a clear visual).

When the slide comes up on your laptop, you don't need to look back at the screen. Be confident that the slide is correctly displaying on the screen. The headline of the slide on your laptop reminds you of the key message you need to deliver. Refer to how the visual supports the message and use any builds on the slide to help tell the story to the audience. When you are done this slide, move on to the next slide. It is much easier to confidently deliver a message when you know there is only one message to recall on each slide, and the headline summarizes it for you.

Plan for stops along the way

Most GPS systems will tell you what time you will arrive after starting your trip. Have you ever noticed how it almost always takes longer than that initial estimate? That's because there are unplanned stops along the way: restroom breaks, food stops, and scenic lookouts to take in. If you are scheduled to arrive somewhere and only set aside the time that the GPS indicates, you will likely arrive late because you haven't taken into account the stops along the way.

It is similar when planning the content for your presentation. If you have been given thirty minutes on the meeting agenda for your presentation, how much content should you prepare? Less than thirty minutes worth. Why? Because you need to plan for discussions and questions along the way. How much time should you set aside for this? It depends on the group and the topic. This should be part of your analysis in the P section of the GPS approach. Look at the audience members, their interest in the topic, and your past experience with them or similar groups. Then determine how much of the time should be allocated for stops along the way. With certain groups I know I will need perhaps as much as 15% of the time for questions. With other groups or topics I know that there will be very few questions and I may only need 5% of the time for questions and discussion.

Recalculate the route if necessary

When you are using a GPS system and you make a different turn than it recommends due to traffic patterns, construction, or you just missed the turn, the GPS recalculates your route given your current location. Presenters need to be prepared to do the same during their presentations.

During your presentation, you may identify that the route you planned isn't working for this audience. Perhaps something has changed at the last minute that has made them focus on a different aspect of the topic. Maybe new information was just published that changes what is needed for the audience. It could be a number of different causes.

In these situations you will have to do what the GPS system does and recalculate the route for the audience during the presentation. If this happens, you will be very glad you followed the GPS approach in planning your presentation. With that as a foundation, you can quickly re-assess where the audience is and what the best route is at the current moment.

When you start down this new route, remember some of the techniques that can now help you use your prepared slides in a different way. Use the Ctrl+S or slide number entry methods to jump to any slide in your file, including hidden slides. This is helpful when your new route includes some of your planned content in a different order. For content that you don't have slides for, use the period key to display a black slide and bring the focus to what you are sharing without a visual distracting the audience. If none of your slides apply, just turn the projector or TV off.

Recalculating the route during the trip is never easy and is often not enjoyable. Once the shock has worn off after the presentation, take some time to assess the causes, how you responded, and what you would do differently next time. None of us will respond perfectly each time, but viewing the situation from a more calm position afterwards often leads to good ideas for the next time it happens.

Changing the destination

In rare situations you will realize during the presentation that the destination you need to take the audience to is different than what you had planned. When this happens while using a GPS system, we just enter the new destination and let it calculate the new route. In the middle of a presentation, it isn't quite so easy.

This is likely to happen when a last minute change in circumstances occurs or a previously undisclosed situation is revealed. These are items that are almost impossible to plan for in advance and call into question the entire goal of the presentation. You may sense this when you walk into the room, during the first few minutes when it appears people are totally distracted, or it is apparent from the first few questions that are coming from a totally different direction than you anticipated.

What can you do in these situations? Like using a GPS, the best thing to do is pull over and stop. Go to a black slide and stop the presentation. Admit you are feeling that there is something going on in the room and check to see what you have been observing. Discuss it with the group and decide how to proceed. It may be that you can quickly resolve the issue and continue with your presentation, although that is likely not the case in these sorts of situations. Use the GPS approach to plan the time together with the group. Once you decide on a new destination and overall plan, review if any of your slides can be used. Use black slides and the slides that fit the new plan to move forward.

These situations are never easy and are often very uncomfortable. I included this section because by reading about it, you will be more prepared if it happens to you (and I hope it never does).

CHAPTER TEN

Putting this into practice

Like any new approach, the GPS approach for planning your presentation will take some time to become the default way you start preparing for a presentation. Here are some ideas on incorporating this approach into your work.

Your highest priority is to keep your job

In almost every workshop I deliver someone will say that they think these ideas are great, but their boss has a specific way of doing things and isn't very open to new ideas. What should you do if you find yourself in this situation? I always remind participants that I realize your highest priority is to keep your job. By this I mean that if your boss requires you to do things a certain way, you have to do what they want if you want to keep your job. That may sound harsh, but it is the reality for many professionals today.

What you can do is influence with examples of what the future could be like. Share makeovers I or others have done showing the changes that could be made and find out what your boss thinks of them. In many cases a boss wants ideas to appear as if they thought of them. Don't be surprised if they come back weeks or months later with this great new idea to change presentations that looks exactly like what you showed them in the past. Praise them for the idea, make the changes, and keep influencing with more examples. It may take a long time, but it is a good way to influence change while keeping your job.

Overcoming common obstacles

As you start using any new technique or approach, you will run into obstacles. Here are some common ones that my workshop participants have shared and my advice on overcoming them.

"I don't have time to do all this!"

Don't try to make all of these changes at once. Make small changes each time you prepare a presentation. Maybe start with 15 minutes on the goal, present situation and steps. Perhaps start with writing headlines for your existing slides. Maybe one slide that has a visual instead of a list of sentences. Changing everything all at once is overwhelming. Take small steps and celebrate the positive changes you see and encouraging comments you receive.

"I need a lot of text to remember what I want to say"

It is good you recognize that memorizing a presentation doesn't work very well. Keep in mind that it is easier to remember your key messages when you only have one message per slide that is summarized in the headline. If you need some more reminders, feel free to create some speaking notes. There is no law against using notes, in fact, I have been speaking professionally for over 18 years and I still use notes every time I speak. Some presenters use the Speaker Notes section of each slide in PowerPoint and either print the Notes pages or use Presenter View to see the notes on their screen. What I prefer is to print my slides as a PDF file and add annotations to view on my tablet while I present. Try different methods to see which works best for you.

"If I remove the details, I can't answer their questions"

It is good that you want to be well prepared for your presentation. Start small by removing just some of the details and use the Before, After, or Behind opportunities to make the details available to the audience. See what happens. When you find that the audience gets along just fine without the extra details, you will have the confidence to remove more details next time.

"My boss wants a lot of text or a spreadsheet on the slide"

As I said earlier, you need to do what your boss requests. But take the opportunity to make some small changes within the parameters they have set. Use the eight strategies to tighten up the wording of the text. Show an example or two of how shorter text points are more powerful and will make the message clearer for the audience. For spreadsheets, review the reasons I shared earlier as to why spreadsheets end up on slides. Look for opportunities to show your boss different ways to present insights instead of measurement or performance results. Assure them that the spreadsheet will be a backup slide that is easily accessed if needed. They may not agree right away to make changes, but trust that the ideas are at least percolating in their mind.

"I don't know how to create a specific visual"

Almost everyone is self-taught at PowerPoint. We learned from others in our jobs and don't know all the techniques possible. It has taken me many years to learn the skills I use to create effective slides. If you want to learn a specific feature of PowerPoint, the best website for free tutorials is www.indezine.com. To create some of the visuals you see in my presentations or on my website, consider purchasing my Implementation Guides that have step-by-step instructions for many of the visuals I use or my other resources on creating effective visuals.

What to do if you are asked to create only one slide

The advice I have given you in this book will lead to more effective presentations that will likely have more slides than you have used before. A significant challenge comes when your boss asks you to create only one slide summarizing a certain topic.

Busy executives are dealing with so many items that they don't have the time to wade through all of the details of every issue. They need their staff to provide just the most important information required for them to understand the issue and make decisions related to it. That is why they ask for one slide, not a full presentation.

Once you understand what the executive really needs, it becomes easier to figure out how to create that one slide. First, realize that the slide they are asking for is not for a presentation. It is more of a document that they can quickly review and be up to speed on the topic. So the one slide will not necessarily observe all of the best practices for slides in the same way as a slide intended for a presentation.

I suggest that you can still apply the same GPS approach as explained earlier. If you can distill the topic down to one point you need the executive to understand, create a slide that has a headline summarizing the point and a visual that illustrates the point as described above.

If you have more than one key point you need the executive to understand, divide your slide into sections. You can divide a slide in up to four sections if needed. Treat each section as a slide on its own. Write a headline summarizing the point and create a visual that illustrates the point. The text will be smaller than it would be for presenting to an audience, but since this is a document, that is fine.

If you need the space, remove the overall slide headline space so that each section can be a bit larger. Once you divide a slide into sections, the text and visuals tend to get quite small, so you want as much space as you can get for each message. To make each section stand out, I suggest using light dotted lines to separate the sections of the slide. This way, the executive will know what content supports which message on the slide.

When you are asked for only one slide by an executive, remember that they are really asking for a one-page document. Plan the message(s) you need to communicate using the GPS approach. Use the space on the slide to communicate the message(s) the executive needs to know. Approach each section of the slide like its own presentation slide, with a headline and visual to make the message clear. It is not the ideal communication vehicle, but one that staff are increasingly being asked to prepare.

Change 10% of a regular presentation at a time

Many business professionals have regular presentations they deliver. It could be a bi-weekly project update presentation in engineering, it could be the monthly financial summary to management, it could be weekly call center statistics, or it could be a monthly sales update. If you have been delivering this presentation for a while now, you have set expectations with that audience. You need to consider this when making changes to your presentation.

At this point in the book, you likely have a number of changes you want to make to your presentations, from better structure, to headlines, to new visuals. You are probably excited to implement all of these ideas in your next presentation. I caution you not to do so.

Why? Because your audience can't handle that rapid pace of change. If you show up at the next meeting with a totally different look to your slides, you will likely run into strong opposition because people usually can't handle a large change all at once. You may be told to go back to the previous look, however ineffective that is, and never make changes again. You will have lost the opportunity to make improvements in the future.

So what will work? What I suggest to my workshop participants is to change no more than 10% of your slides at a time. If there are two new slides in a typical twenty slide presentation, the audience will feel comfortable because most of what they are seeing is familiar. They can handle a change that is small and not drastic. Next time you present, change another two slides. The new slides from the first time are not new anymore, so the audience doesn't perceive it as a large change each time.

Will this approach take a long time to upgrade all the slides in your presentation? Absolutely. If you do monthly presentations, it will take almost a full year! But you are making the changes at a pace that the audience will accept. I think it is more important to get to a better final presentation than it is to push the pace of change that makes the audience uncomfortable and may make them resist your improvements.

Start small, let the audience get comfortable with the new look at a reasonable pace, and you will reap the benefits of more successful presentations personally and professionally.

Index

This index provides a more detailed outline of all the ideas in the book with page references so it is easy to locate the specific idea you read or want to find.

Training Services

I develop and deliver customized training sessions for teams that deal with data who want to create and deliver PowerPoint presentations that have a clear message, focused content, and effective visuals. The ideas get implemented because I share practical approaches and show makeovers of actual slides the team is using so they know it applies to them.

How is the training that I deliver different from other services you may consider? Typical presentation training and consulting falls into one of three areas: technical PowerPoint courses, stand up presentation skills, or design focused training. If those are the skills you need, that is great. I can suggest experts in these areas. What I provide is different. You learn an approach to planning a clear message, strategies to focus your content, and a way to select and create effective visuals. You practice the techniques in PowerPoint so you can immediately start creating more effective presentations in less time.

On my website you can see details of what is covered, read testimonials, and see my extensive client list. When you are ready to take the next step in making your PowerPoint presentations more effective, contact me.

Phone: (905) 510-4911 (Eastern North America time zone)

E-mail: Dave@ThinkOutsideTheSlide.com

Web: www.ThinkOutsideTheSlide.com